STOMP, DINOSAUR, STOMP!

Ankylosaurus
an-ki-loh-sore-us

Triceratops
try-seh-ra-tops

Iguanodon
ig-wah-noh-don

Brachiosaurus
brak-ee-oh-sore-us

Velociraptor
vel-oss-uh-rap-tor

Plesiosaurus
plee-see-oh-sore-us

Diplodocus
dip-lod-oh-kus

Oviraptor
oh-vee-rap-tor

Pteranodon
ter-an-oh-don

Stegosaurus
steg-oh-sore-us

Tyrannosaurus
tie-ran-oh-sore-us

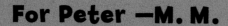

For Peter —M. M.

For Henry, Elinor, Ollie, and Milly —A. A.

ISBN 978-0-545-30265-4

Text copyright © 2010 by Margaret Mayo. Illustrations copyright © 2010 by Alex Ayliffe. All rights reserved. Published by Scholastic Inc., 557 Broadway, New York, NY 10012, by arrangement with Walker Publishing Company, Inc. SCHOLASTIC and associated logos are trademarks and/or registered trademarks of Scholastic Inc.

12 11 10 9 8 7 6 5 4 3 2 1   10 11 12 13 14 15/0

Printed in the U.S.A.   08

First Scholastic printing, October 2010

Art created with cut-paper collage; typeset in Billy Bold

Margaret Mayo   illustrated by Alex Ayliffe

STOMP,
DINOSAUR,
STOMP!

SCHOLASTIC INC.
New York Toronto London Auckland
Sydney Mexico City New Delhi Hong Kong

Mighty Tyrannosaurus

loved stomp, **stomp**, **stomping,**
gigantic legs **striding,** enormous jaws **opening,**

jagged teeth waiting for guzzle, **guzzling!**

So **stomp,** Tyrannosaurus, **stomp!**

Immense Diplodocus

loved swish, swish, swishing,

long tail **flicking** and fast whip, **whipping**,

enemy **surprising** and—*smack!*—scaring.

So **swish**, Diplodocus, **swish!**

Crested Pteranodon

loved glide, glide, gliding,
spreading wide wings, circling, rising,

higher and higher, swooping and soaring.

So glide, Pteranodon, glide!

Fierce Velociraptor

loved hunt, **hunt, hunting,**

in fearsome packs **running, racing,**

hooked claws ready for quick **pouncing**.

So **hunt**, Velociraptor, **hunt!**

Sleek Plesiosaurus

loved zoom, zoom, zooming,

sturdy paddles swooshing, flapping,

neck lunging, teeth showing—**snatch!**—fish **trapping.**

So **zoom**, Plesiosaurus, **zoom!**

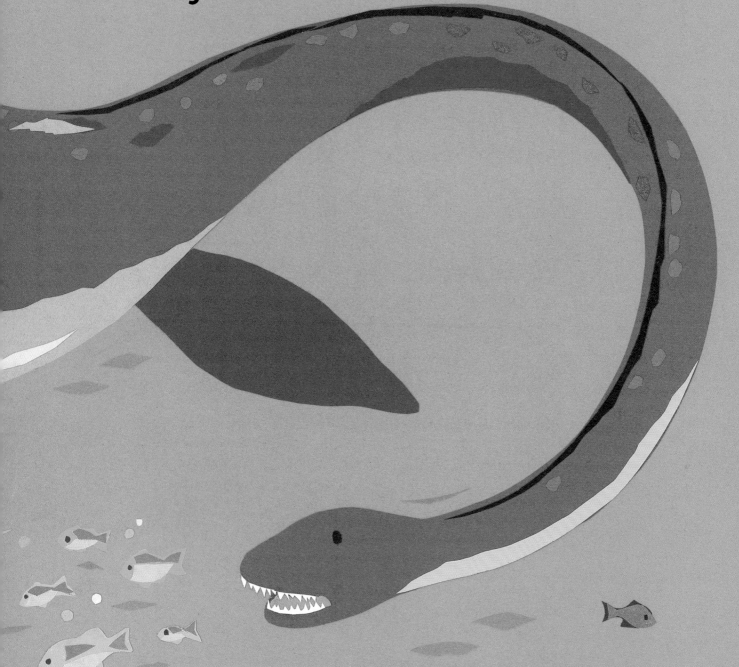

Tough Ankylosaurus

loved whack, whack, whacking,

tail-club **swinging**, battles **winning**,

Massive Brachiosaurus

loved gulp, gulp, gulping,

leaves **picking**, mouth **stuffing** . . . no **chewing!**

Fast **eating,** hungry, hungry giant . . . more food needing.

So **gulp**, Brachiosaurus, **gulp!**

Wrinkly Triceratops

loved charge, **charge, charging,**
thumpety-thump! Huge feet **pounding,**

horns **jutting**, and—*wham!*—head-butting.

So **charge**, Triceratops, **charge!**

Stiff-tailed Iguanodon

loved chomp, chomp, chomping,

tough plants grabbing, cutting, and biting,

chewing, mashing, and noisy grinding.

So chomp, Iguanodon, chomp!

Feathered Oviraptor

loved guard, guard, guarding,

soft sand shaping, snug nest making,

eggs protecting, until—cric-crac!—babies hatching.

So guard, Oviraptor, guard!

Fantastic Stegosaurus

loved stroll, **stroll, strolling,**

tiny eyes **glaring,** spiky tail **waving,**

showing off big curvy plates . . . and looking quite amazing!

So stroll, Stegosaurus, stroll!

Imagine the creatures in a grand parade—

with no fighting allowed and no one afraid!

Some **plodding,** some **swooping,** while others just **romp,**

and Tyrannosaurus leading . . .

STOMP! STOMP! STOMP!

Ankylosaurus
an-ki-loh-sore-us

Triceratops
try-seh-ra-tops

Iguanodon
ig-wah-noh-don

Brachiosaurus
brak-ee-oh-sore-us

Velociraptor
vel-oss-uh-rap-tor

Plesiosaurus
plee-see-oh-sore-us

Diplodocus
dip-lod-oh-kus

Oviraptor
oh-vee-rap-tor

Pteranodon
ter-an-oh-don

Stegosaurus
steg-oh-sore-us

Tyrannosaurus
tie-ran-oh-sore-us